sticky fingers

sticky fingers

andrew campbell

Beyourownvogue
PUBLISHING

Beyourownvogue Publishing
a division of TrendsByTrenton
www.beyourownvogue.com

for the ones i love

on a journey to find myself i
lost myself to find myself

contents

God and i

i was blessed to see
another day that
wasn't even
promised, for that i
am thankful

today i felt like giving
up, but i was
reminded God
wouldn't put more on
me than i can bear

make me over
make me new
take it out Lord
things that are not
like you
cleanse my heart
Lord mold my
mind with your
help i will be fine

- *honest prayer*

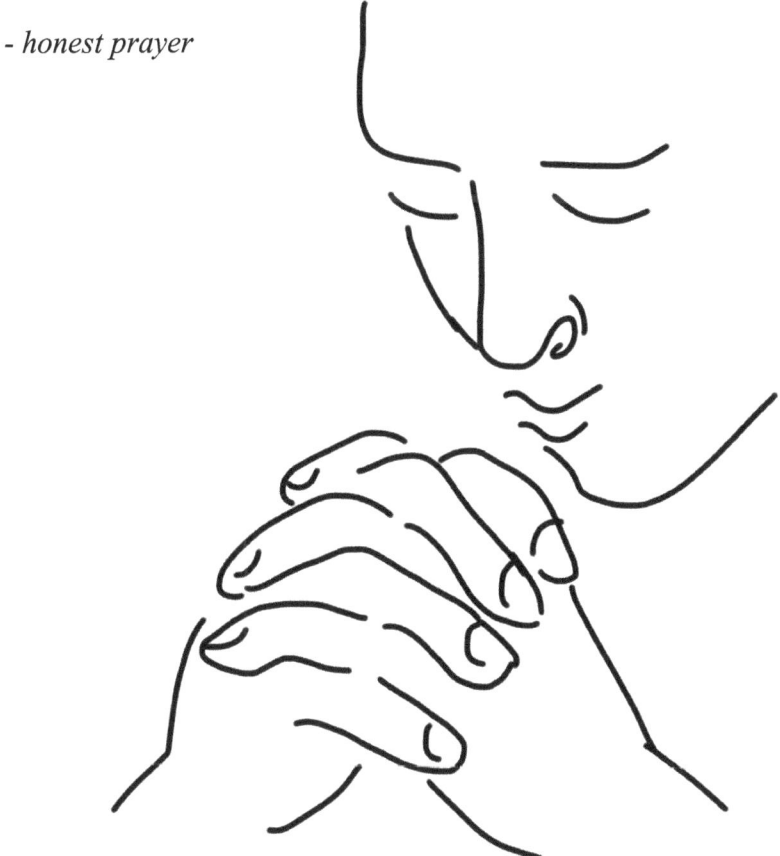

she whispered in
my ear and told
me *tell him yes*
all God wants is a
yes

it's a favor when
sin rejects you yet
we still chase it

throw up your fears
and come running to
him she said

i am with you and
will watch over
you wherever you
go, and i will bring
you back to this
land. i will not
leave you until i
have done what i
have promised you.

- genesis 28:15

i'm ready for the change i
don't want be the same
Lord i need something new
Lord come in and do
whatever you want to
i need you to heal me
i need you to fix me
Lord make me new
i need you to take out all
things not like you

i'll use your words
to magnify your
name your words i
shall proclaim

the world is fast can't
make up my mind
things are changing
all of the time, but i
understand that the
joy of the Lord is
mine

your friends turned
their back on you
said they'd always
be true

- *hallelujah anyhow*

your love is
unconditional , is that
why i still choose to
do wrong

dancing in an open
field rain falls from
the heavens gently
washing me clean,
i'm so glad he laid
his hands on me

i was down in my sin
had no joy had no
peace within then
God showed up and
he stepped right in
thank you Lord for
being that friend

Lord i really need
you to help me get
it together

i often try hard to be
the best i can be
whenever i take one
step something is
always two steps a
head of me

for the rest of my
life i owe you

God, my
youth is
yours

thank you for
always loving
me

though i'm not
worthy you still
give me new
mercy day after
day

keep your head up
trust me i know it
hurts, the race is
not given to the
swift nor the strong
but he who endures
until the end.

- still small voice

your grace is sufficient
for me
your grace is ever
lasting
your grace is all that i
need
your grace is
everything

i asked God to
change my heart to
make it tender again
i asked him to use
me

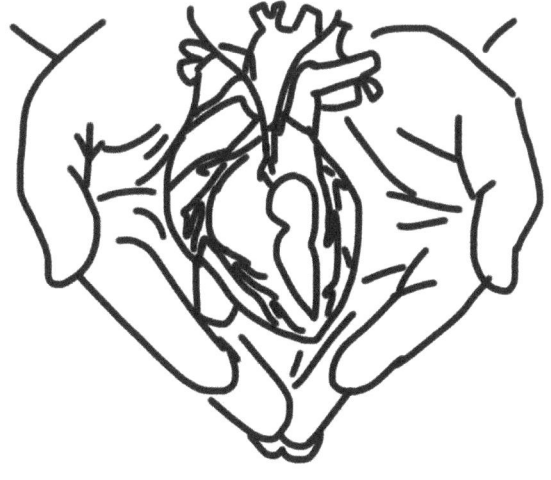

let all bitterness, and
wrath, and anger, and
clamour, and evil
speaking, be put away
from you, with all
malice

-ephesians 4:31-32

judge not, and ye
shall not be judged
condemn not and
ye shall not be
condemned forgive
and ye shall be
forgiven

-luke 6:37

when i think of the
goodness of Jesus
and all he's done for
me though i'm not
worthy of being left
in the land of the
living he made death
behave

tears descend
from my eyes
unknowingly
as i watch you
weep for his
touch
it warms my
heart to see
worship go
forth

if i would have
gotten it back then
i know i would
not have been
ready for it,
he may not come
when you want
him but he's
always on time

i've put everything
before you
when i was taught
to put you before
everything

when God blows
he blows a fresh
wind

- holy ghost fire

you asked me was i ready
to give it up
you knocked on my door
and i only cracked it
you went seeking and i
tried to hide
you told me cast up my
cares and i kept them in
the basement
you told me you'd wipe
away all tears from my
eyes; and there shall be no
more death, neither
sorrow, nor crying, neither
shall there be any more
pain: for the former things
are passed away.
i opened the door and let
you have your way

it crawled instead of
walked it was
desperate for sin , i
had to relinquish the
thoughts of flesh in
order to let him back
in

no something,
someone, or it can
take away my
smile

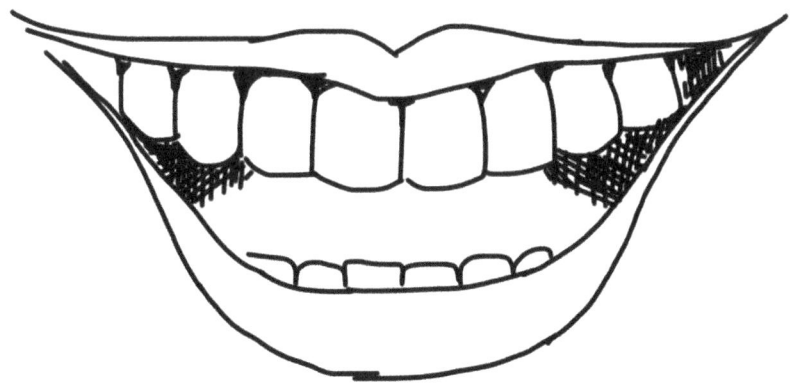

Lord i'm
desperate for
you

seek the
kingdom of
God

to know
God is to
know
forgiveness

he who the son sets
free is free indeed

tears plunge
from the lens
of site softly
soothing my
dirt stained
cheeks
washing away
everything
keeping it
from being
clean

ever just take a
moment and say
*God you are
amazing ,*

sticky fingers

i get chills
when i feel
your presence

andrew campbell

the more i
call on your
name the
better i feel

you've worked
miracles right before
my eyes and i still
pretend to be blind

you never left my
side even when i
made you look bad

i have to go
through friday and
saturday in order
to get to sunday
i have to go
through the
breaking, beating,
and pressing in
order to become
who i'm destined
to be

- *resurrection*

i was lost in my sin
i was down i was weak
the more i dug deeper
the more i strayed away
seemed like all hope
was lost for me , but i
had a praying mother
she got down on her
knees and she prayed
she asked the Lord *can
you save him on today
fill my child with your
precious holy ghost take
away what his flesh
desires most*

- mamas prayer

its hard walking
in faith , but its
not impossible

today is
your day

you begin to leap for
it and before you can
come down something
will be there to push
you back up

i whispered in
secret and you
heard every word

i feed you
apologies like
meals throughout
the day
to double the
problem i don't
give you water to
drink the excuses
away

you broke
every chain
and i was
still shackled
at my own
cost

i had something
but had nothing
until i met you

i was a library with
few books, the
books i had were
full of blank pages,
you took look at
me and filled them
with complete
sentences

i can't see it right now
but i know it's on the
way

-faith

i might get up slow
, but God sees my
effort

i knelt down and
cried like i had
never cried before
i cried out for peace,
self love, and
happiness and for
the first time in a
long time they were
real tears

i was never
ashamed to say i
believe in you i
was only ashamed
of the sin i did
knowing it didn't
reflect you

trust in the LORD
with all thine heart
and lean not unto
thine own
understanding.
in all thy ways
acknowledge him,
and he shall direct thy
paths

-proverbs 3:5 - 3:6

yea, though i
walk through the
valley of the
shadow of death,
i will fear no
evil: for thou art
with me; thy rod
and thy staff they
comfort me

psalm 23

i felt like nothing
though i was born
of royal blood

you're so much
bigger than any
battle i face why do
i try to fight them
on my own

i was more
afraid of what
man might think
rather than the
creator of man

i am the lips your
words pour from
i am the body that
acts in your will
i am the soul that
gently connects to
you, i am your
vessel

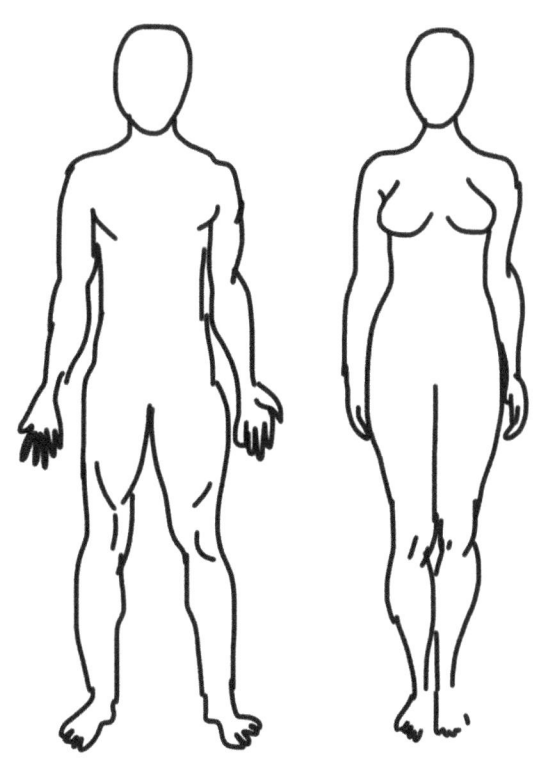

let all bitterness, and
wrath, and anger, and
clamour, and evil
speaking, be put away
from you, with all
malice

Ephesians 4:31

i learned to forgive fire for leaving its burn scares stained on my back and you forgave me for burning you purposely while laughing in your face

---

And when ye stand praying, forgive, if ye have ought against any: that your Father also which is in heaven may forgive you your trespasses

Mark 11:25

you called
and i
answered

but seek ye first the
kingdom of God,
and his
righteousness; and
all these things
shall be added unto
you.

-matthew 6:33

i and i

life is full of ups and
downs it may give you
the run around if you
know its secret touch it
will hurt but not that
much

i am not a fool
though i play one

late at night i check for
monsters under my bed
never catching them.. i
pull the covers toward
my chest taking deep
breaths, i peek below in
fear to see myself

society may have you down situations may have you bound, we ask ourselves am i to big or to small or maybe to short or to tall my skin isn't light enough why is my skin is so dark and rough always looking at a half empty glass and always coming up last , *didn't anyone ever tell you you're beautiful no matter what they say from the souls of your feet to the crown of your head, so next time you feel like you're not good enough look your self in the mirror and say i am so strong and tough you're beautiful no matter what they say you're beautiful and wonderful in every way*

imagine being cut by a
thousand pieces of glass
still managing to hide the
wounds with a smile and
the clothes you have on
the only hope is that one
day the sharp objects
miraculously refract and
the wounds heal

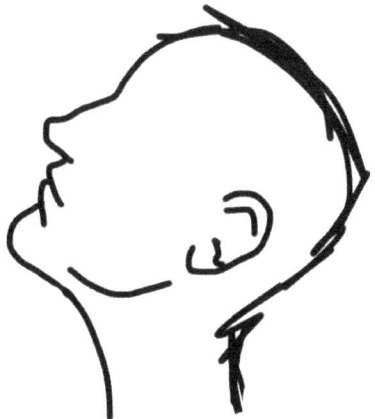

there is
triumph in
loving me for
me

- words to self

i'm a weed in a
field of daises
you find me
useless, but i am
truly beneficial in
my own way

when life gave me lemons i made
apple juice

life gave me ups and down and i
turned them around

life gave me head aches nothing
but sorrow and pain

life gave me you babe and i
wouldn't trade it for the world to
gain

life gave me the thrill you seek
sneaking out at *2am* while
everyone else is sleep

life gave me the run around so i
got tired and i just shut down

life gave me a family and i'm
much better than i use to be

life gave me heart break and i'm
angry and bitter at the one i use
to date *(let it got)*

life threw me a curve ball and i
kept it

life gave me love
life gave peace
life gave me sorrow
life gave my hope for tomorrow

- life

waking on monday
morning i feel the need to
stay in bed no one knows
what i did all last week
and now this is the day it
all repeats so i'll be the
best of the worst day ever
and i'll tape a smile on my
frown so i can get around
your questions cause all i
want is my bed all i need
is my bed

- *mondays*

i've never been the
one to talk with my
fist

time heels all
wounds, but they
open and close on
cue

ever been so
happy you could
cry

thats a good feeling

i hate purple hats,
but my favorite hat
is purple

i said i loved you
but i lied thought
saying it would
make it real

i said i love you so
you wouldn't leave
the sad thing is it
didn't stop you

i found joy in
myself for my
self

i have so much
pride in being
black

i like the chase , but
when the prey is
caught i don't care for
eating anymore

- *liking you*

i am learning
how to love
myself the way i
wanted everyone
else to love me

twirling under an old
oak tree leaves kiss the
bottom of my bare feet
the wind clings to me
as tears flow purely
down my bark colored
cheeks *thank you Lord*
i whisper

i thought by filling
you where i was
empty i would
become full
i was a fool to
think so

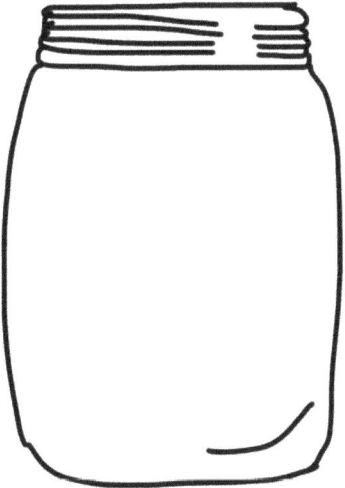

i'm afraid of getting
hurt is just a substitute
for i don't wanna be in
a relationship

she is gone but she
use to be mine

not in my 21 years of
living having ever felt
so confident in my
looks until today.

i've watered my
self with tears i've
cried from days
with no sunlight
yet i still grow as if
there was

don't lose what
you can't replace

you can't replace
what you don't
have

how can you walk
away from something
and still come back to
it *recycle*

i shut my mouth
closed my eyes and
wished you away
like you wished i'd
stay non of it
happened

- the cycle

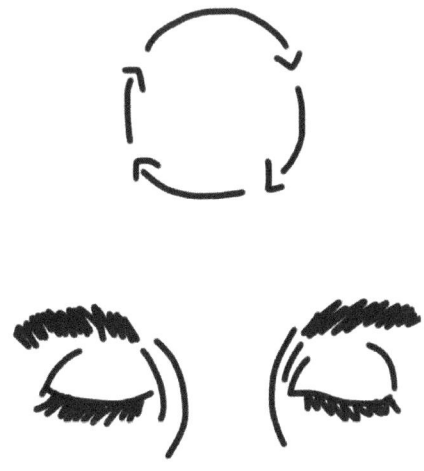

if you don't
jump you'll
never know
how hard the
fall is
if you never
fall
you'll never
know how
much stronger
you'll be
when you get
up

its easy to say
harder
to do the
right
determination
you can do
what you
want to do

if you love what you
do the money will
come to you

- *career*

i said i'd change
but that was
fifteen years ago

he's so hard yet so soft
i can't be harder than a
bolder in a pillow case
makes it a pillow

no matter what
mask you wear
you're still you
underneath it

i know you're afraid
but do it anyway

- to the younger me

i am a pencil that
dances across lose
leafs of paper
leaving stains of
my past behind

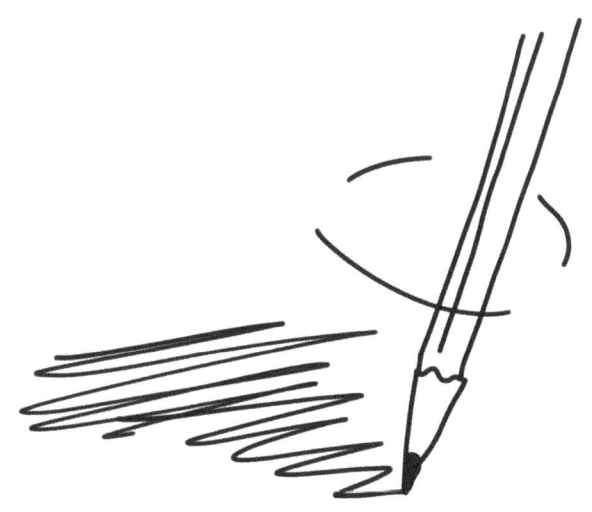

its ok not
to be ok

there is life beyond
how you're feeling
right now

never shy away from
the monstrousness
thats the only way
people will
understand what you
go through

i faced my
insecurities and
their power over
me was released

sitting under
the stars i feel
at peace
driving into
nowhere i
feel free
being able to
express my
self is me
being me

its easy to talk
about in theory, but
it takes a bold
confidence to take
a stand

the worst thing about
knowing good from
evil is choosing
something you know
will kill you
is it the thought of the
near death experience
or just the thought of
knowing you're
already dead.

i won't let you
know how pathetic
you were for
blocking me
but with my empire
growing you'll see
me anyway

how can you miss
something that doesn't
because it did exist it
just went extinct

i tell myself things
will get better due
to the fact it can't
get any worse

its hard to choose
between right and
wrong when you've
been addicted to the
pleasure of being
immoral

i keep the
television on late at
night to feel less
alone even though
i am alone

i won't tell you i'm not
doing ok
i won't tell you i've
been feeling weak
i won't tell you i've
been crying long
nights
i won't tell you how
much i long for peace
of mind
i won't tell you about
my selfish goodbye

i'm going to make
mistakes and i'm
going make more
mistakes i'm going
to learn from those
mistakes to make
more mistakes

love tugged at the tail
end of my coat when
depression hid
secretly in the pockets

the guy who
stares back at me
in the mirror i do
not recognize
he's tried to be
someone else for
so long he's
invisible

i tried to drown the
thought of you by
drinking you away
smoking only left you
lingering in empty
space popping only
slowed the fact that
you'd be there when i
came to

i have my doubts
but doubt turns into
determination if
you really don't
want to be stuck
where you are

i'm afraid to ask
because deep down if
they asked me i'd say
no

andrew campbell

i thought i'd be able
to straighten my
self out if i ironed
out all of my issues

i pretended to have
words when i only
had a letter

i felt the need to be
what society
deemed fitting
it only made me
unhappy

though i was broken i
used my bones as
symbols to heel the
minds of those in
need of guidance

i often still feel
lost with the map
in my hand

the more you're
around someone the
attractive they become
i never had a taste for
olives until it was all i
had

shadows dance
around my bedside
as i lay resting
they tempt to grab
me but a still voice
says no

i've swept it under the
rug for so long i've
gotten splinters from
gripping the broom

love sheltered me
when sorrow
rained many nights
for that i will
forever be thankful

them and i

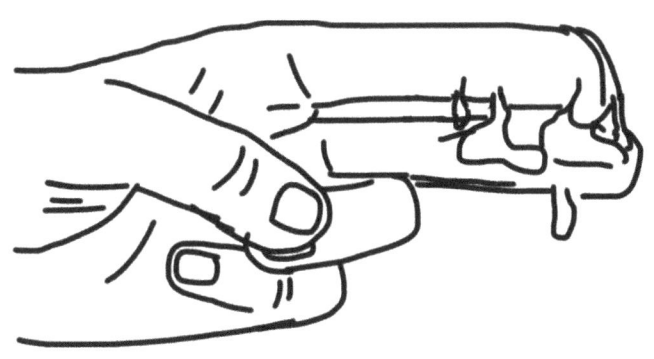

you brought me
dark clouds of gray
but i just said *hey*
it'll get better if we
can just stay
together

-relationships

you were just like me
so i let you see all of
me i let you in

- *the first time*

i want to be
with you and
not be with you
all at the same
time

you and i the perfect
two no one else can
do what we do
you and i were
meant to be lets go
run away with me
its me and you no
one else but us two
its you and me free
to be free

i could sink into
the sound of your
voice as it wraps
around me making
me feel wanted

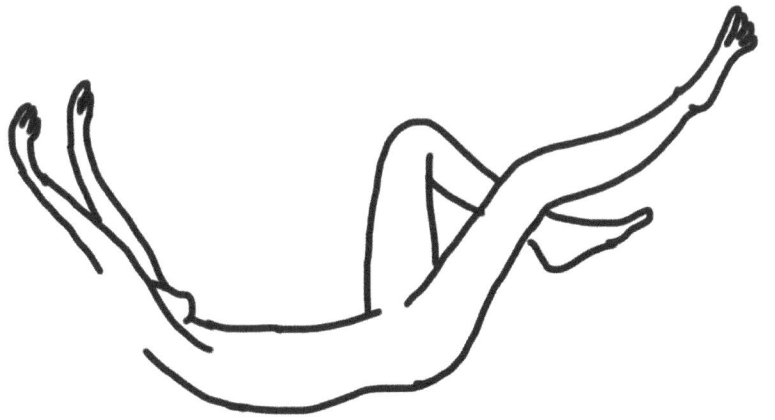

you *i love you*
me *i lust you too*

people that have
don't flaunt
people that don't do
drinking water is
normal to those
who drink it daily

you drive me
mentally insane
now let me show
you how it feels
let me get behind
the wheel

it was two of us
and i still felt alone

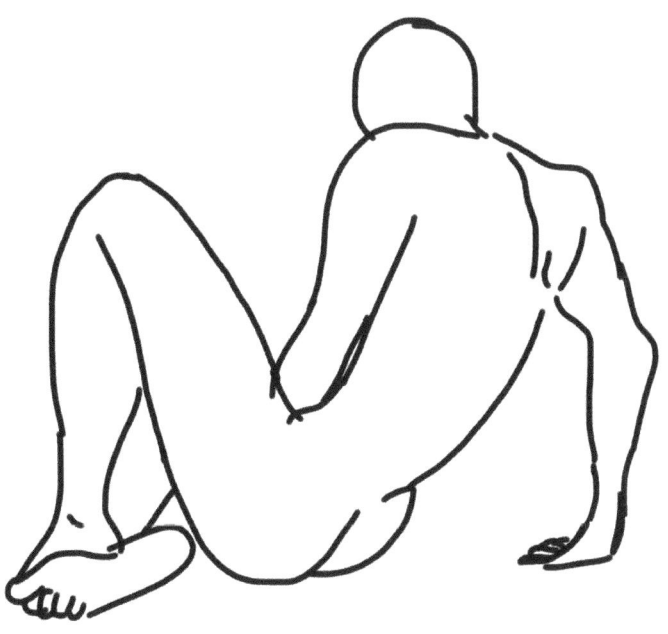

three girls five guys
twin beds pushed
together truth or dare
a broken pelvic bone
one heck of a night

-college

as a child i would
cry out for my
mother just to
make sure i could
still hear her voice

you've been blessed
with a lot of gifts you
can be anything you
want to be just
remember keep God
first he will never fail
you

-mom

if you stay then you just stay
if you leave then you just leave
if i cry i'll wipe my own eyes
i will not force what does not
need force not anymore

-letting go

when you inspire
people are inspired
when you lead people
follow
when you're original
you can't be replaced

i watched them
laugh, she held his
arm and all he
could do was smile

-thanksgiving '16

i liked you when you
didn't like me
you liked me when i
didn't like you
when we did it was
awkward because we
both were use to
playing games

- reality

nothing is sweeter
than when we
make angelic
music with the
instruments we
were born with

do you want it
because you want it
or do you want it
because you see it

- aunt

i could tell you missed me
from the way your eyes
grew after every lingering
word that sweetly poured
from my lips
i could hear your
heart beat as it skipped
towards me
you opened your arms i
gently extended my hand
and smiled

- to my ex lover

they start to
recognize you when
people they admire
recognize you

you discovered
scars i tried to keep
hidden rather help
me find bandages
you pick at sores
inflicting pain
purposely

- insecurities

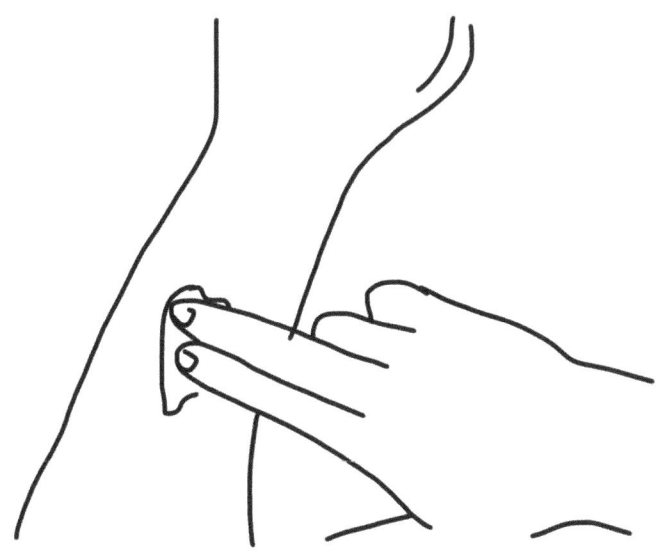

we argued day and
night never once did
we not, they were so
regular i looked
forward to them

the worse thing
about missing you
was when i left you
didn't even notice i
was gone

the toy you picked up
when you'd lost your
others
the game you played
when you'd been
defeated
the heart you loosely
held in the palm of
your hands
the water you drank
when you had nothing
else to sip on
the tool you used to
fix a bike that wasn't
even broken

- used

you kissed me and
for the first time i
felt nothing

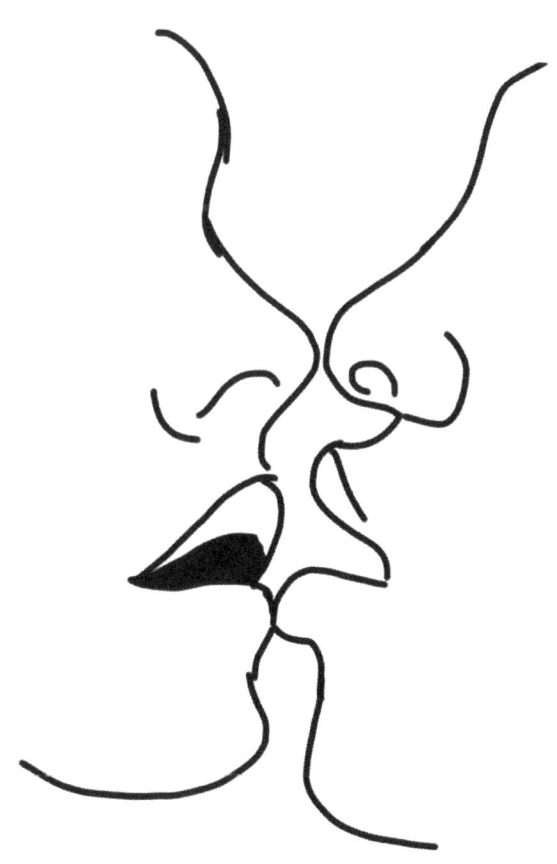

i know that we are
through but i can't
help myself but
surround myself
around you
i'm allergic to peanuts
but i love peanut
butter , i'll eat it until
i die

- loving you

andrew campbell

your heart beat is
music to my ears

you won't make
love to me unless i
set the fee

andrew campbell

i gave you my
heart but you kept
it hostage

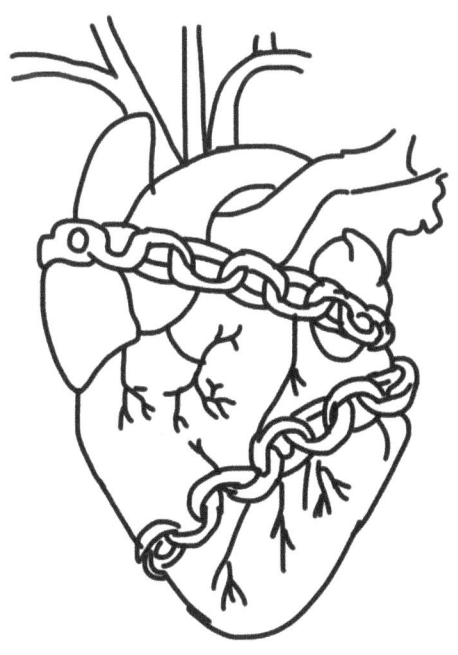

sometimes i imagine
it was all a dream and
you just moved
faraway as a cruel
joke to withdraw from
the reality of never
seeing you again

- sunset, 2013

ever since you left
i've felt your scent
caress the inside of
my nose every
place i've gone

you can't tell me
you've been
telling your
friends about me
i'm so proud of
him you say *hes*
gonna be it i can
feel it but walk
right past me in
the hall way

you talked about
me now you talk
about me

i was mad at you for
wanting him and not
me

to the person
reading this ,
understand and
know you're
beautiful and
wonderfully made.

we were in love
we fell out of love
you say since we fell out
of love we were never in
love, if i fill a glass of
water to the top drink it
empty does that mean it
was never full

put yourself in my shoes. they are nice and spacious , but if you wear them for to long you'll get blisters , they'll begin to swell up and if you don't have the right antibiotic you'll lose your feet

you may think its easy stepping into my situation , but if you're not equipped with the knowledge to handle the issues that come a long you'll go crazy

everything you
did was like a
splinter small
yet painful

you watched me
put blood sweat
and tears into my
empire,
notwithstanding
you said nothing
,not that i cared its
just you stared for
so long it was
required

you're the reason for
someone's reason

i've aways felt your
love more when
you were gone

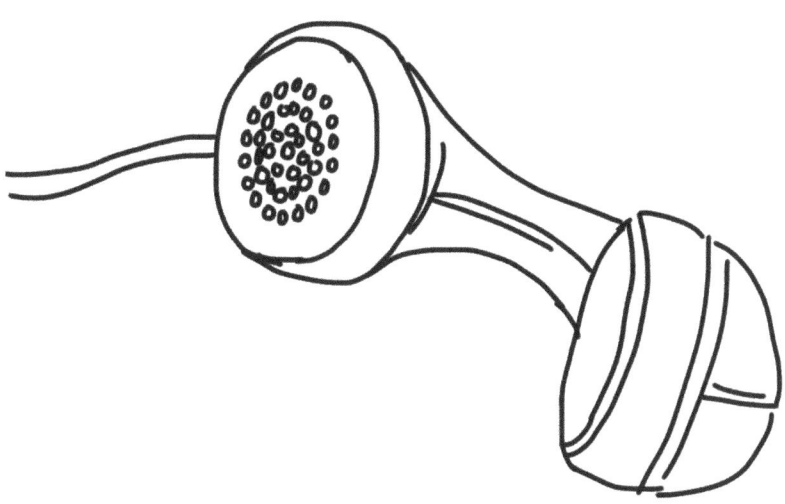

you told me to test
the water only in
hopes i'd drown
when i stepped in

your love brings
me peace in the
mist of confusion

you remind me of
every mistake i've
ever made

you were just a
mannequin only
displayed to show

i stepped away not to
hurt , but to heal. i
weep for your loss ,
but i weep for my
gain

i told you i was
scared and you
cured my hiccups

i yearn for the thought
of not having to see
you without glasses

people are different
when you live
together

i like what
you do but i
don't like you

you encouraged me
to be the me you
wanted me to be

family will fight
lions and bears
for you while
friends fear to
squash a spider

your personality
shined so bright
your skin glowed
leaving light in
dark places

i took endless
showers to remove
the scent you
smeared on my skin
from late night
shack ups

trying to digest
dreadful memories
is like eating sand
only to have it
bolted like rocks
on the ocean floor
after consumption

it's not me it's
definitely you
i can't spare
feelings i don't
have

on days like this i
long for the sugared
smell of your skin as
it brushes up against
mine

you unfolded me
like a napkin at
dinner time you
wiped your mess
on me then threw
me away

i pray against any thought
of feeling useless i pray
against depression,
suffering, fear , anything
hindering you from getting
closer to your reward i pray
you keep walking though it
seems far i pray you find
peace and love
in Jesus name i pray amen

Andrew Campbell

I've always been different. I was not your average guy. I did not like football, baseball, wrestling, and bragging on how many girls numbers I got at that party. Everyone around me made A's and B's . On the other hand I made C's. I was not perfect, but I worked hard at my weaknesses. For me Fashion, drawing, singing, dancing, filming was my passion. Because of that I was talked about. In school I was teased constantly. "Why do you talk like that?" "Are you gay?" "Act like a boy!" "Go outside!" "You're weird""Where's your man at?" PEOPLE made me feel like a creature, like I wasn't good enough. I cried many nights in my room. Of course I did not tell my parents because I did not want to disappoint them. Even if they saw fit to taunt me. I had family down my throat saying "don't draw girls all the time" "Play football" "Put some bass in your voice". I could not figure out what I was doing wrong. I felt like a science experiment one who was beautiful to the Creator, but a freak to the public. Over time I began to internalize what people said about me as a result I changed. I took what they said as the truth. I lost what made me unique. Attached to my hands and feet were imaginary string. I was a puppet in a horrible joke. I looked myself in the mirror staring back at me was a face I no longer recognized. One day my Mom called me into the living room. She told me I was different from Everyone else. God blessed me with enormous talents and I should use them all. I remember her saying you are unique like no other. Not knowing what I was going through she spoke words of encouragement. As only a mom could, she knew what I was going through without a word being told to her. With her words the chains that bound me were broken. Through color of gray gently faded away I prayed on the situation and felt so much better. That different and unusual kid came back. I realized I was different for a reason. I learned to be my self no matter what people said. I am original and cannot be replaced. Being myself has gotten me a lot of positive attention. Academically I have been working harder than I've ever been. God created everyone for a reason. We are blessed to stand out for different purposes. I realized that I am more than what people make of me. I am what my father says I am, and I am a child of a King.

Lightning Source UK Ltd.
Milton Keynes UK
UKHW01n1439100818
327056UK00002B/13/P